AF316996

IBERIAN RAILS

LAST DAYS OF THE OLD ORDER

The railways of Spain and Portugal on the eve of modernization

VOLUME 1: CATALONIA

The first of three volumes that illustrate a tour of Spanish railways and tramways in summer 1963, just before the traditional rail scene — which resembled that of North America around 1920—was swept away by modernization. Volume One focuses on Catalonia, including broad-gauge steam activity, the narrow-gauge "toy trains" of Gerona, the remarkable rural tramway of Mataró, and Barcelona with its huge city network and American-style interurbans.

BY
Fred Matthews

Gotham Books
30 N Gould St.
Ste. 20820, Sheridan, WY 82801
https://gothambooksinc.com/

Phone: 1 (307) 464-7800

© 2023 Fred Matthews. All rights reserved.

No part of this book may be reproduced, stored in a retrieval system, or transmitted by any means without the written permission of the author.

Published by Gotham Books (June 6, 2023)

ISBN: 979-8-88775-244-0 (h)
ISBN: 979-8-88775-345-4 (p)
ISBN: 979-8-88775-245-7 (e)

Because of the dynamic nature of the Internet, any web addresses or links contained in this book may have changed since publication and may no longer be valid.

The views expressed in this work are solely those of the author and do not necessarily reflect the views of the publisher, and the publisher hereby disclaims any responsibility for them.

DEDICATION PAGE:

To the memory of

Laurence Russ Veysey

1932-2004

Outstanding Historian

Enthusiastic Railfan

Stormy Petrel

BARCELONA
Horta
Montaña Pelada
Iglesia Parroquial
San Gervasio Monte Putchet
El Turó
Sarriá
Estación
Las Corts
Sans
Hostafranchs
Barrios de Montjuich
Montjuich
Montaña de Montjuich
Castillo de Montjuich
Cementerio del Oeste
Gracia
Ensanche
Campo del Arpa
S. Martin de Provensals
Clot
La Llacuna
Pueblo Nuevo
Sección Marítima
Estac. del Norte
Estación Francia
Estac. d. Villanueva
Catedral
Universidad
Seminario
Cárcel Modelo
Velódromo
Matadero
Mercado
Cementerio
Conv. de Capuchinos
Iglesia
Conv. de Elisabets
Inst. Freneopático
C. Provin. de Maternidad
Asilo S. Juan
Conv. Carmelits
Colegio de Jesús y Maria
Cuarteles Bruch y Gerona
P.P. Maristas
Ntra. Sra. del Carmelo
Ntra. Sra. d. Coll
Sta. Madrona
Lérida y Zaragoza
Granollers
N.

A NOTE ON THE SPELLING OF NAMES

In 1963 Spain was in the grip of the Franco regime's attempt to eradicate the historic languages of regions like Catalonia, Valencia, and the Basque Country around Bilbao. So, names were Castilianized, sometimes even changed to eliminate regional resonances. With the restoration of democracy after 1975, and the devolution of considerable authority to the Regions, older names and spellings returned.

Since this is historic record, I have given them as in 1963, sometimes with the older/newer form in parenthesis. Names and spellings were a minor example, almost invisible to the tourist, of the pervasive repression practiced by the Franco regime. Those who wish to understand that aspect of the fascinating country we toured should read the great novel by Camilo José Cela called <u>The Hive</u>, about life in Madrid in 1940s.

Super narrow: One of the newer engines of the 75 cm (2'5¹/₂") gauge FC de San Feliu de Guixoles Gerona, built in 1905 by Krauss in Germany (to 1891 design) making up the evening train to San Feliu at Gerona.

CHAPTER I:

ON SPANISH RAILS: NORTHERN CATALONIA

An extensive tour of Spain and Portugal in the summer of 1963 was inspired by a coming-together of several motives. I had just passed the exhausting Ph.D. oral exams at Harvard, and was seeing double after years of intensive reading and very competitive graduate classes. Europe was still relatively affordable, if already not at Arthur Frommer's legendary $5-10 a day. Iberia in particular beckoned, because its broad-gauge railways were still largely steam-powered, though on the verge of modernization. And most important, my old California friend, Laurence Veysey, then a Harvard instructor and always a fervent fan of streetcars and interurban railways, spoke fluent, though certainly not native, Spanish. Having just finished the book that would establish him as a leading historian, <u>Emergence of the American University</u>, he was eager to return to the pursuit of exotic tramways and rural electric railways.

It was already possible to learn a certain amount about the Iberian railway scene. I knew enough to know that Spanish steam locos, and much of the Spanish landscape, were very like the American railway scene still fresh in memory--large, loud engines, operating through dry and often semi-desert terrain strikingly like the American southwest. So, there was far more enthusiastic anticipation than fatigue when, after a wide journey through northern and central Europe, we reached the high point of our summer's rail quest: the broad-gauge network of Iberia (not to mention a wide variety of narrower lines).

Arriving at the French border station, Cerbère, we had immediate confirmation of the special excitement of Iberian railways. We had changed in Narbonne from the old Midi Railway's D.C. electrified main line to a Cerbère train, still steam-hauled using one of the 'Liberation' 2-8-2s built in vast numbers by Alco, Baldwin, Lima, Montreal and Canadian Locomotive to re-equip the damaged French network in 1945-47. These simple, sturdy locos, designed for common usage and easiness of operation, were not small by standards north of the Pyrenees. Loco and tender were 79 feet long, weight was 115.5 metric tons, official top speed 60 mph, though the 65" drivers allowed higher.

One of the SNCF's 2-8-2s left for Narbonne during our wait, and gave us a vivid sense of the contrast between "European" and "Iberian" motive power. It passed a much larger, smooth-sided 2-8-2 of the 5'6" gauge RENFE, or Red National des Ferrocarriles Espagnoles. The RENFE was a government-owned system created in 1941 to consolidate four major and some minor broad-gauge companies left without reconstruction funds at the end of the bloody, destructive Civil War in 1939. Despite inheriting a broken and bankrupt group of companies, RENFE had had little new funding until the late 1940s, except for necessary repairs and replacements. Spain was struggling with savage domestic repression, then ostracism and isolation by the victorious democratic powers after Generalissimo Franco's Axis friends were finally defeated in 1945.

The big semi-streamlined 2-8-2 represented the first wave of RENFE's painful modernization. When money for improvement began to flow again, it went first to new steam power, mostly home-built. Spain, like Britain, had vast coal deposits (often low-grade) but relatively little domestic oil. It also faced a persistent lack of foreign exchange, due partly to Franco's hostility to foreign influences, including capital. Hence, new home-built steam, until external relations improved in the mid-50s as the United States saw Spain as a reliable ally against Communism. Even then, given the masses of skilled, low-paid steam men, construction of steam continued until after U. S. aid (often in kind) and new economic advisors led to a policy of dieselization from 1958.

The big engine that greeted us in Cerbere was the flower of the first postwar construction. Three hundred and forty-two heavy 2-8-2s, of class 141/2101, were built between 1953 and 1960 by North British and (mostly) the four major Spanish builders, Macosa, Maquinista, Eskalduna, and Babcock & Wilcox. They had relatively small drivers, 61" versus the French 141R's 65". Since it was still rare for standard passenger trains to go much over 60 mph, the 141s performed well on the heavy freights and long, infrequent passenger trains typical until the mid-sixties.

Although numerous, the big Mikados were not typical of RENFE motive power--they were some 15% of the 3000-plus steam locos, more than balanced by several hundred ancient teakettles built before 1890. Most of these senior citizens were 0-6-0s or 0-8-0s, built as road engines but now serving modest days on not-very-busy local switching duties, but you could still see them around Valencia on medium-distance local passenger and mixed trains. RENFE's most numerous types were some 680 big 4-8-0s of various designs, built with government aid during the 1920s. There were also over 500 2-8-0s, and over 200 each of 0-6-0s, 4-6-0s, 0-8-0s, 2-8-2s and 4-8-2s, plus a variety of other types including tank engines and a few Beyer-Garratts and compound Mallets.

The best English-language introductions to Spanish railways in the 1960s are L.G. Marshall's <u>Steam on the RENFE</u> (Macmillan,1965) and two books by D. Trevor Rowe: <u>Railway Holiday in Spain</u> (David & Charles, 1966); and <u>Spain and Portugal</u> (Continental Railway Handbook, Ian Allan, 1970). Rowe gave some basic statistics for the broad-gauge RENFE system which was decreed in 1941 and operational from 1943. The RENFE was the consolidation of four sizeable and several small private companies; it had about 7126 route-miles, along with extensive unfinished sections that had been delayed, often destroyed, during the bitter Civil War of 1936-39. By the late 1960s, route-mileage had risen to 8563, as several long lines were completed--Zamora-Ourense, Madrid-Burgos "direct," Cuenca-Valencia. Track on main lines had improved, but there were still thousands of miles of light, jointed rail.

Steam was still the dominant motive power in the early 1960s, with over 3000, but diesels were arriving in substantial numbers, so that by late 1968 there were 700 active steam locos, all now oil-burning, as against about 650 full-sized diesels and some 20 TALGO locos. (There were no major closures in the Sixties; the decrease in available locomotives was allowed partly by new railcars, partly by diesel's greater availability). Electrification had been expanding slowly for decades; by 1968 there were about 360 electric locos running over 1900 route-miles, plus some 3-phase units recently retired from an isolated electrification at Almeria in the far South.

Passenger rolling-stock was beginning to be standardized with modern double-truck metal-bodied cars. At the end of 1963 there were 1462 wood-bodied coaches (some of the double truck ones fairly new and comfortable) and 954 modern metal cars. Over 900 four-wheel coaches ran in 1949; 316 in 1967. The wooden cars came in a great variety, so that some local trains seemed to have no two similar cars. Completing the roster were automotors--diesel or gasoline railcars. About 30 railcars, turned out in brilliant silver, dated from 1935-41, and Fiat had supplied fifty 3-car TAF (Tren Automotor Fiat) sets from 1952 for daytime express service. The low-slung, ultra-lightweight Talgo, the great Spanish contribution to modern railroading, was about to emerge from infancy; but in 1963 only a handful ran Madrid-Irun and Madrid-Barcelona expresses, less than daily. Such was the wonderfully diverse "Red" (network) of Spain's broad-gauge railways.

The modern 141's were running their last months south from the French border, since electrification was nearing completion. Our 2-8-2 would come off the train, with us, at Gerona (in Castilian; now Girona, in Catalan), 43 miles south. It was already mid-afternoon as we chuffed along south, at a typically leisurely pace despite modern equipment--perhaps RENFE was planning a dramatic speedup with completion of the electrification.

We were not going far--the first sizeable Catalan city, Gerona/Girona, boasted not only a giant cathedral and picturesque riverside housing, but two of Spain's numerous narrow gauge 'private' railways (that is, not operated by the RENFE).

Big Brother: An American built SNCF 2-8-2 departing Cerbre, the French border station, passing a 10-year-old RENFE 2-8-2 which has brought in the connecting Barcelona train from Gerona.

At Llansa, about 6 miles south of the French border, another modern 2-8-2 brings in northbound Train 1111, the 10.25 Tranvia from Barcelona, while our southbound #1104 waits for it to clear the single track. About 3:15PM

Modern, if still some wood-bodied, coaches on #1111 from Barcelona at Llansa, not far from the beaches of the Costa Brava. Train #1111 (#2141 from Barcelona) has taken 291 minutes for about 100 miles, with 30 stops.

Gerona (Girona in Catalan), town of ancient stairways, and three different railway gauges.

West of the RENFE, the meter-gauge Gerona-Olot's train #102, the 11 AM Automotor to the industrial town of Olot, some 34 miles inland, loads at its depot.

Gerona-Olot railcar and trailers take off for Olot in a typical Spanish slim- gauge station scene.

Like a Chirico painting the traditional Catalan village of Llagostera, Sunday 1 PM. Other days, other hours, might have been a bit livelier.

Super narrow: One of the newer engines of the 75 cm (2'5' 1/2")
gauge FC de San Feliu de Guixoles Gerona, built in 1905 by
Krauss in Germany (to 1891 design) making up the evening train
to San Feliu at Gerona.

Smokey Start

SFG's 18.45 Mixto to San Feliu charges out of Gerona, with a coach built in 1891 by Maschinesbau in Nurnburg, Germany

Bucolic terminal---SFG #3, built by Krauss in Munich in 1890, waits on the 12.15PM Correo in Gerona

TORRES
LICOR
nacal
NET
OLCHON-MUELLE
SEMA
LINE
Sintetico Señal
PINTURAS

Central Gerona, along the Rio Onyar, looking east to the massive
Gothic cathedral, built from 1312 over three centuries.

Llagostera, Sunday 1 PM.

Thirteen miles and 56 minutes from Gerona, the little Krauss
0-6-2T pauses for light maintenance at Llagostera, with
Correo No.8.

1891 coaches on SFG's Mixto #7 at Llagostera, in from
San Feliu de Guixotes at 2.15 PM

Engine change on the broad gauge, a modern RENFE 2-8-2 waiting to replace electric on a morning train at Gerona

Busy Station: Gerona RENFE, late morning, with expresses passing. #114 from Port-Bou arriving a few minutes late, meeting semidirecto 1103 which has averaged about 40 mph, with five stops, over the electric line from Barcelona.

Since they were of different gauges, there was no connection between the two private lines, separated by the RENFE mainline. Of the 33-mile meter gauge Olot-Gerona line we saw only a two-car automotor depart for the slow trek into the hills southwest. Because it was steam-hauled and more picturesque, we focused on the super-narrow 75 cm (2'5 1/2") gauge FC (Ferrocarril) de San Feliu de Guixoles a Gerona, opened in 1892 and absolutely unchanged in the intervening 70 years.

San Feliu was already a coastal resort on the booming Costa Brava; but tourists didn't use the tiny, hard-seated wooden coaches. Even had they known of it, the crawling schedule---25 miles in around two hours---would have repelled them. There were four mixed trains and one Correo (postal train) per day, hauled by one of six Krauss 0-6-2T's built in Munich between 1890 and 1905.

On our first evening in Gerona, we photographed Train 10bis, Mixto de Verano (summer) on its excited, and crowded, 18.40 departure from Gerona. Next day we rode the 12.15 Correo as far as Llagostera, an unaltered, picturesque 18th-Century town with dirt streets, about halfway to San Feliu. We were beginning to face a problem that would persist: Iberian branch and short lines were so slow and infrequent that it literally took all day to ride them. The line as far as Llagostera was not exciting, undulating through scrub forest and dry farmland. And, as serious 1950s-type academics-in-training, we had a date with Gerona and its architecture.

The presence in Gerona, a city of 36,000 in 1950, of three separate railways, on three separate track gauges, resulted from Spain's tangled and troubled railway history. The broad-gauge main lines began first, from the 1840s, with major construction financed by foreign capital between 1850 and 1880. Although the evidence is inconclusive, the broad gauge was probably chosen for military reasons, to make invasion from Europe more difficult. In the 1840s two major invasions, by Napoleon and then by the restored French monarchy in 1822-3, to crush a liberal government, were still within living memory. The choice may have made a major difference a century later-- legend has it that in 1940-41 Hitler had planned to send an army across Spain to capture Gibraltar, until his generals warned that the break of gauge at the French border was a major problem.

Spanish narrow gauges came a generation or more after the broad, as local and foreign interests agitated for cheaper ways to connect towns and exploit natural resources. Away from the few large cities and rich Huerta (irrigated plain) along the Mediterranean coast, there was an impoverished traditional society, with poor roads, few canals, and difficult transport.

The early broad-gauge system, like the earlier royal roads, was a hub-and-spoke network focused on Madrid, still reflecting the Habsburg monarchy's drive to create a centralized nation out of several regional societies. Much of the land, therefore, was still without railways, though often with rich resources waiting for exploitation, and always with local elites convinced that a railway would be their lifeline to prosperity. But capital (mostly foreign) was cautious, except where (as in Asturias and at the great Rio Tinto complex in Andalucia) foreign corporations created little enclaves of their own, to mine for export.

In this endemic state of capital starvation, anything that could cut costs substantially was a godsend, and a sizeable literature extolling the narrow gauge appeared (as in the U.S. at the same time). Between 1870 and 1910 a series of overlapping, sometimes contradictory laws gave, or permitted, state and regional subsidies to "secondary" and "strategic" railways, the latter a way to justify subsidies in the name of national defense.

At first most of these secondary lines were meter-gauge, but as costs even there proved daunting, in the 1880s a new campaign began for ultra-narrow gauge, 75 cm (¾ meter, or 2′5 ½″) gauge. These unstable-looking "toy trains" proved surprisingly successful and long-lived, as the Gerona-San Feliu line proved. But their slow speeds created severe vulnerability once roads improved.

Originally, most of the narrow-gauge lines were privately operated, though often with local government participation. As road traffic began to bite them, as early as 1930 in some areas, those considered still useful were taken over, or subsidized, by government, and called <u>Estado</u> lines, though still using their old names. As weaker lines closed, equipment was shifted around. There were still several major private narrow-gauge lines in 1963, notably along and inland from the Bay of Biscay in the north, where industry was heavy and thick. After the mid-sixties, government limitation on rates led to losses, and then to either closure or takeover by the new government narrow-gauge company directorate known as FEVE (Ferrocarriles de Via Estrecha). Many FEVE lines folded in the late Franco years (1960-75), when highways had priority; but most of the North Coast system and at least one other managed to survive.

Classic rural tramway: the Mataró a Argentona out in the fields on one of its half-hourly trips. People seemed to ride end-to-end on this 5 3/4-mile line, built in the 1920s. Two of the line's six boxy cars, which resembled those in several other cities, were in service at any time.

CHAPTER II:

TRACTION WONDERLAND: MATARÓ AND BARCELONA

Leaving Gerona around 12.30 in a 2nd-3rd class local, we headed towards the Catalan metropolis, Barcelona, 62 miles west. But not without an essential stop. At Mataró, some 40 miles south of Gerona and now part of greater Barcelona, there was an incredible tramway survival, the rural line from the industrial town of Mataró across open fields and along lanes to the village of Argentona. There had been hundreds of such lines around Europe in the 1920s, especially in France. But by 1960 there were a handful—the Ebelsburg St. Florian in Austria; the wonderful Sintra Atlantico in Portugal most of which survives today; two lines out of Granada, and the <u>Tranvia de Mataró a Argentona</u>, S.A. formed in 1926. Like several other Spanish tramways, it opened, or was electrified, only in the mid-1920s when the Primo de Rivera government extended the electric grid beyond the few largest cities. Typical of many Iberian tramways, the TMA operated with its original equipment, six boxy 4-wheel cars, using two or three each day for a 20-minute ride every half hour over the 4.5 km of metre gauge. Mataró, "a grim industrial town" (Baedeker) had 30,000 residents in 1950; Argentona was too small to rate a mention in my 1950 Atlas. Recollections, and photos, suggest the little cars carried decent loads—perhaps because we were there during one of Spain's four peak hours, morning, noon, midafternoon, and evening. Trees were being chopped down along the line's narrow road, suggesting a widening that would kill the tramway, as Mataró itself was engulfed in the massive expansion of Barcelona's suburbs.

Since Gerona we were on an electrified line, the northern outpost of the Barcelona suburban system that was gradually wired, first at 1500 volts then 3000, from the early 1950s. The RENFE favored electrification, but was constrained (as in Britain) by high costs and a government that regarded railways as less important than roads. So, until the early Sixties, electrification came in bits and pieces, with steeply-graded freight lines and busy suburban routes the main targets. Our final jaunt into Barcelona's impressive Termino station was on an energetic, modern Swiss-looking EMU.

We arrived in Barcelona's grandiose Norte or Termino station, built by the old Madrid Zaragoza & Alicante in the 1890s near the waterfront east of the old center. Termino had been named Franca or Francia in earlier years when Catalan identity was more tolerated; since Franco's death the old names, and the old spirit and energy, have revived to make Barcelona one of the most admired cities in the world.

Barcelona (population 1.27 million in 1950) was not only Spain's wealthiest and most cosmopolitan city, but also the capital of Catalonia, once an independent kingdom, later a partly-autonomous region with its own language. And with a certain condescension towards the proud Castilians of the central highlands, who had tightened their rule over the centuries until the culmination under Franco, who hoped to obliterate regional identity and patriotism altogether. Compared to the beautiful but sometimes rather dead and paranoid cities of the central table-land, Barcelona seemed almost Parisian in its bustle and friendliness.

Our hotel, the Gran Via, carefully selected, was on the tree-lined Gran Via de Cortes Catalanes, between the old quarter and the late-19th Century Eixample. From our window we watched a steady procession of vintage and modern trams trundling past. Aside from its famous buildings and colorful street-life, the "Manchester of Spain", its industrial and trading capital, was still, just, home of the country's most varied and extensive network of trams and fascinating suburban electric lines. (We also noted that standard sight of Spanish cities, the eighty- or ninety-year-old steam locos, 0-6-0s or 0-8-0s, that simmered away quietly in the sun down by the port, between infrequent switching duties.)

Six of the suburban lines were RENFE's, like our train from Mataró, with 1958-model Swiss-style dual voltage (1500 and 3000 DC) EMUS, some using an underground station at Plaza Catalunya, near the Gran Via. But there were also three municipal metro lines, and two non-RENFE systems, one narrow gauge--the FC Catalanes, electrified close in but still steam-hauled on long rural extensions. Our prime target was the legendary FC de Catalunya, a standard (4'8 ½") gauge system boasting what since earlier in 1963 had been one of only two lines using American -style heavy interurban cars. Some of these classics had been built by J.G. Brill in Philadelphia in 1917, others to the same pattern in the FC-C's shops in the early Twenties. For a few years these cars ran through Barcelona's streets, but the frequent accidents impelled subway construction on the inner end, and from 1929 they served a 6-track underground terminal at Plaza Catalunya next to the narrow-gauge and municipal systems and one RENFE terminal. Most of the 31 Brill-type motors and trailers had been rebuilt (some more than once) to look more modern, but they retained classic heavy traction sound.

The Mataró à Argentona trams out in the fields on one of their half-hourly trips.

From the new world, almost: built in the company shops (1922) to a Brill design,
FC de Catalunya #27 trails a train for the textile city of Tarrassa as it leaves Sarria,
on Barcelona's outskirts

Blue Tram #10 at the lower terminus, where it connected to the Municipal tramway and a short branch of the Sarriá/Catalunya system.

Morning light on the Gran Via de Cortes Catalanes, with a recently-arrived PCC from Washington, D.C.

Rebuilt PCC on route 46 has just left its terminus at the
University, and heads east on the Gran Via, then
northeast to Sagrada Familia and Plaza Ibiza. Here it's
crossing the Paseo de Gracia

COMEDIA
EL TRAPISONDISTA
RENFE

Another 800-class car from the mid 1920s, on Route 39 to Barceloneta, near the harbor, passes the Palacio de Justicia and the Arco de Triunfo, northeast of the old city centre. The Arco was built for an 1888 fair, and celebrates Barcelona itself, its history and survival from Castillian overlordship.

Gaudi's memorial: the 82-year-old architect was hit by a tram in 1926, Perhaps by a car like unrebuilt 839, one of 84 built by Gerona in 1921-23. Sagrada Familia was on a group of routes extending northeast from the center.

Another boxy 800 class car from the early 1920s on the short-turn route 60, which looped beyond Sagrada Familia and then around the big-city-centre circle.

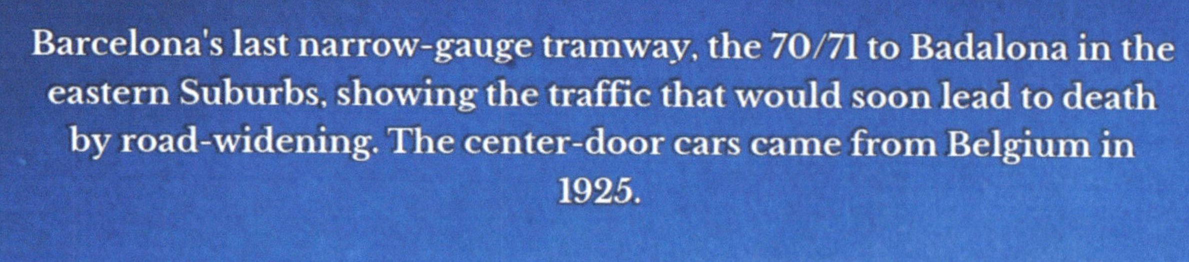

Barcelona's last narrow-gauge tramway, the 70/71 to Badalona in the eastern Suburbs, showing the traffic that would soon lead to death by road-widening. The center-door cars came from Belgium in 1925.

MINISTERIO DE LA
EL PASO

The monorail at Tibidabo amusement park, looking across the Southern half of Barcelona to the Parc de Montjuich.

One of the Tibidabo tramway's 1905-era cars at the lower funicular station.

Car 9 of the Tibidabo tramway toils up the hill, with central Barcelona part hidden at center-left and Montjuich at right.

CINZANO
CINZANO

In sight of the Mediterranean at Mataróthe--Mataró-Argentona tram. Much of Europe had overflowed with rural tramways like this from about 1910 to 1930. Spain, which had only three or four, was poor enough, long enough, to allow these photos.

Along the Gran Via, a double-truck motor leading, with the old university buildings behind.

A mid-1920s car crossing the Gran Via for Plaza Catalunya out of the Eixample, the district laid out in the 19Th Century, and then on past the Tibidabo tramway.

A mid-1920's car crossing The Gran Via for Plaza Catalunya, coming from The Eixample, the district laid out in the 19th Century.

FELISOL

Simmering teakettle on the Barcelona waterfront-RENFE 030-2605, one of 42 0-6-0s built by Hartmann from 1882 to 1890, awaits a switching job under the eyes of Columbus (at the Plaza de Colon, in the background).

Not matching: one of the Norte's last and heaviest class of 0-8-0s, built by Henschel in Germany in 1910, sits on the Barcelona waterfront, with the tender from a 2-8-0.

Barelona's beloved symbol: Antonio Gaudi's Sagrada Familia, begun c. 1900, still unfinished in 1963

The U.S.-style walkover rattan seats are hidden as a set of Brill-style Interurban lays over at the Tarrassa terminal, ready to leave for Barcelona

The one-car route 12 shuttle, which connected to Route 64 at Plaza Sarria, in the northwest, and clanked a few blocks to Plaza Duque Gandia, had trouble coping with motor traffic.

New Swiss-style RENFE EMUs at Mataró, on the hourly-or-better suburban service to Barcelona.

At the Plaza de Colon near the waterfront, a rebuilt former
narrow-gauge train, originally Belgian-built around 1925,
on Route 57 to Collblanch in the northwest.

Broad boulevards threatened tramways: Barcelona's oldest survivors, an open motor car built by Gerona in 1906 near the Columbus statue, on Route 55 northwest to Sans

The motor car dated to 1906, but the "vintage" trailer to 1951! Looking towards Montjuich; the cars will turn right (inland) here. The line to the left was closed later. At the right, the medieval shipyard now a prime tourist attraction.

The Brill cars, with their powerful motors, operated hourly through services on two fairly long routes to the textile cities of Sabadell and Tarrassa. There was more intensive service, using newer and slower cars, on the first few miles out of Barcelona, and a new (1952), 1-mile urban branch to Avenida Tibidabo. Like many Spanish rail lines, this had been partly build decades earlier, but the project was abandoned during the Civil War and the years of austerity that followed.

At Avenida Tibidabo this underground line met one of Bacelona's tramway treasures—still now surviving into the 21st Century, since it was always a tourist line. This was, and is, the "blue tram" or Tibidabo tramway, a 1.2km line that twists up into the hills from the city system (and later the Catalunya underground) to the foot of a funicular that takes pleasure-seekers up to the large, popular amusement park atop a mountain with extensive views over the whole city. Other rail lines, including a small monorail, entertained visitors in the park. The blue tram up to the funicular's base station was operated by two or more of six single-truck cars built locally in 1904-1909. Unlike many small Spanish tramways, these are not the original equipment, but were added for an extension into the hills that was later abandoned. The slow ride up to the funicular gave a vivid glimpse of the mansions of the Barcelona elite of around 1910.

If the blue-and-white symbolized the pleasures of Tibidabo, then the warm, bright red-and-cream cars of the large city system symbolized (consciously or not) the lively, welcoming spirit that Barcelona maintained even through the repressive rule of the austere Castilians. Although some routes had begun to close after municipal ownership in 1958, this was still a dense and busy system, indeed the largest and busiest in Spain, with modern and modern- seeming cars along with hundreds of boxy single-truckers clanking along the principal boulevards and probing out into nearby residential areas.

As of 1962, Felix Zurita's essential <u>On Rails in Barcelona</u> (London: Light Railway Transport League, 1963) estimated no less than seventeen car types, including about 180 single-truck motor cars and 80 similar trailers. About half of these were the boxy units built between 1906 and 1926; the rest were semi-streamliners rebuilt locally by Maquitrans or the company's shops from 1943 to 1955. Girona had built 50 traditional double-truckers in 1926, and Maquitrans turned out about 160 streamstyled "PCC" cars (using traditional electric equipment) after World War II. "Genuine" PCCs from Washington, D.C. were still arriving in 1963, bringing a more subdued two-tone blue paint- scheme that was just beginning to spread to the older fleet. All in all, some 600 motors and trailers were available for service on the standard-gauge system.

In 1962, by Zurita's count, there were no less than 31 separate routes, traversing some 72 miles of single track on about 39 miles of streets. Many of the routes overlapped extensively, or were halves of two-way loops. The core of the system was a very large two-way circle around the old city, using broad boulevards created in the 19th Century when the walls were torn down to integrate the expanding new quarters. Some routes made the entire circle, but most turned partly along, around ceremonial fountains or triumphal arches, before branching off to the north and west, some to make short loops in established neighborhoods, others venturing further out into 20th Century suburbs.

A few lines that had penetrated the old city were gone by 1963, but there were two remaining anomalies. Up near the Tibidabo tram, Route 12, a little one-car shuttle, ran along a very narrow street from (in the then-required Castilian spelling) Plaza Sarria to Plaza Duque Gandia. This little route struggled with large vehicles that blocked it frequently. Just surviving northeast of the center was the last remnant of a narrow-gauge system. This fragment extended out into the industrial suburb of Badalona, with some side-of-road operation; it used narrow center-entrance cars built in Belgium in 1923-25. Heavy road traffic soon doomed this service, as it would the rest of the system a few years later.

When we visited in 1963, the future of the Barcelona tramway seemed fairly optimistic. There had been a plan formulated in the mid-Fifties, for extensive motorization along with major Metro extensions. Three or four routes from the 1962 list had closed by the summer of '63. But the conversion plan was long-term; as of 1963 there were plans to extend three routes out into newer suburbs that had no planned Metro extensions. And 67 surplus PCC streamliners were in process of arriving from Washington D.C.

And yet: only five years later the system had shrunk to a couple of routes, soon to vanish. It is not conclusively clear what had changed. Some reasons seem obvious. Motor traffic was increasing rapidly, fostered by government policy to build a major motor-vehicle industry and consumer economy. The operating environment of Barcelona's tram routes also encouraged motorization—most ran either along narrow streets where they blocked traffic, or along very broad boulevards which looked to planners like dream sites for future high-capacity trafficways.

These reasons may be sufficient. But there is a railfan legend, which may not be absurd. As the story goes, sometime in the 1960s the elderly Generalissimo Franco decreed that tramways were dangerous "Communist" enterprises, hotbeds of subversion, and must be purged. It is certainly true that not only Barcelona but other urban systems vanished rapidly in the late 1960s. And local officials were appointed by Madrid until late in the Franco era. It's also true that transport workers had been one center of the socialist and anarchist movements that made Barcelona's 20th Century history so stormy, and bloody.

In a broader sense, there was (and is) in conservative circles a hostility towards big, collective rail-based operations in general, since their "interlocked-ness" makes them necessarily collective and centralized, likely to have strong unions. This may have colored the minds of Franco's economic advisors, who did favor a road-based economy in the 1950s and '60s. It was possible to operate buses on a more decentralized basis, thus fragmenting and weakening the power of unions. Such attitudes certainly shaped policy in Britain under Tory governments, and in some Latin American countries.

In a less apocalyptic manner, the official history of Barcelona transport by Marc Andreu lends some support to this interpretation. Andreu notes that "the tramway and Metro companies had a corporatist social policy that was very challenging to the Franco regime," and that "economic pressure" from local and multinational companies encouraged the Madrid-appointed Mayor, who was close to Franco's modernizing officials after 1957, to push for full motorization and, indeed, to encourage private transport over all. At any rate, the little blue Tibidabo cars were Spain's sole tramway survivor for a quarter-century, until modern light-rail routes began to open.

www.ingramcontent.com/pod-product-compliance
Lightning Source LLC
Chambersburg PA
CBHW042323140726
48196CB00015B/709